A to Z Marketing

An Essential Guide for the Small Business

and the Social Enterprise

Jon Obermeyer

Tomol Press

2017

Copyright ® 2017 Jon Obermeyer and Tomol Press

ISBN 978-1976395949
First Edition

All rights reserved. No portion of this book may be reproduced in any form without permission from the author, except for brief excerpts for reviews.

Cover ahoto by author:
Persimmons, Clement Street, San Francisco

Internal photo by author
Duet, San Francisco Ferry Building

Dedicated to Lizzi and her fellow Millenials

Also by Jon Obermeyer

The Reassurance of Ghosts (poems)

The Winter Practice (short stories)

The Low Wire: Meditations on Loss and Creative Restoration (essays)

It Happens That Fast: A Santa Barbara Memoir

Salispuedes (poems)

Centripetal Force (short stories)

Myriad: A Poet's Guide to the Writing Life

Analog: Creativing Relevance Trust and Loyalty in a Digital World (with Mike Lingo and John Miller)

Contents

Introduction	1
The Full Stack Marketer	2
The Technology Tailwind	6
Audience	8
Brand	10
Content	12
Digital	14
Engagement	16
Funnel	18
Google	20
Hyperlocal	22
Insight	24
Juice	26
Keywords	28
Listening	30
Mobile	32
Niche	34
Opportunity	36
Pricing	38
Questions	40
Research	42
Storytelling	44
Target	46
User Generated Content	48
Viral	50
Wants v. Needs	52
Xerox	54
You Tube	56
Zero Cost	58
Further Reading	60
About the Author	61

The aim of marketing is to make selling unnecessary.
- Peter Drucker

Markets are conversations.
- Levine, Locke, Searls and Weinberger

A to Z Marketing

Introduction

Marketing A-Z is an introductory look at marketing for sole proprietors, small business owners and non-profit managers. Designed for individuals without a formal business background, the book highlights and defines 26 core marketing concepts and strategies. It's an ideal refresher for anyone wishing to understand the current state of marketing.

Each chapter is a letter of the alphabet representing a key marketing concept, which I explain in very simple terminology. Accompanying each topic is a blank "Takeaway" page. This is your chance to write down notes that are relevant to your small business or social enterprise. It's an ideal place to formulate "next steps" and organize what resource (person or vendor or software application) might be able to help you.

I don't have a formal business or marketing degree, I've learned these concepts on-the-job and in the trench warfare of being a bank branch manager, a media executive, a grant writer, a seed fund director, a technology services marketing director and the owner and general manager of a trade show and convention services company that supported over 180 events annually in the Southeastern United States.

If you're interested in building out your marketing knowledge, I've included a "Further Reading" list at the conclusion of the A-Z chapters.

Don't be intimidated about Marketing. I had to scratch my head when it came to acknowledging superior marketers I have known in my career. Most people who have a Marketing title just aren't that savvy about it. The majority of what you will read in this book has been culled from authors I've read and direct experience.

I hope you find this book entertaining, useful and inspiring.

The Full-Stack Marketer

Within a small company, the founder/owner will wear many hats: banker, bouncer, janitor, human resources and and customer service. Each role cannot be approached half-heartedly or else service (and product) will suffer.

You can't necessarily ask an intern or your wife's nephew to take on these roles because they are all inter-related. Running a business or managing a non-profit social enterprises means mastering multiple roles, each of equal importance.

Simularly, the Marketing role (one of your Main hats) is now diviied up into six (or more) sub-roles, each with a specific professional type, skill set and tool kit.

To master all these functions is to become what is known as a "full-stack" marketer, a generalist of the highest order (and pay scale).

Taking on multiple roles will mean using both sides of your brain, the logical left hemisphere (analytic, quantitative, rational and verbal) as well as the more creative right hemisphere (conceptual, holistic, intuitive, imaginative and non-verbal).

Make sure you know when to activate which part of your brain in the marketing process.

1, Market Visionary (Investor/Sociologist)
In this role you think constantly about what markets and market segments to pursue. You are constantly reading, observing and listening for the major trends and shifts in consumer behavior and interests. You apply critical thinking to test your assumptions and you learn quickly whether a market is feasible and can support your efforts.

2. Market Researcher (Psychologist)

Dive down to the personal level of market analysis, thinking about individuals and small groups within a market segment, creating market "personas." In this role you obsess over what might make a person interested in purchasing your product, and later becoming a loyal repeat customer who tells others about it. You become an expert at knowing how much people will buy, when they will buy it, and how often. The tools at your disposal include the Internet, business libraries and online surveys like Survey Monkey.

3. Branding Expert (Creative, artist)

Think of this role as your internal "Mad Man," the creative with the beard, man-bun and wacky t-shirt who skateboards to work and goes to Burning Man every summer. This individual knows how to boldly interpret your product or service and express it as a distinctive brand. The Creative also knows how to position the brand, starting with your logo and website and every single "touchpoint" in the user experience.

4. Chief Content Officer (movie director)

This is your inner Steven Spielberg, taking charge on the set, arranging props, herding and motivating the actors and calling the shots. The content developer role involves knowing when to follow the script and when to stray from it and improvise on-site. The director creates exciting, engaging stories that drive customer action and help change behavior. These stories are posted on any number of channels including static ads, videos, web landing pages, social media pages.

5. Marketing Operations (scientist)

Now we switch back to the left side of the brain and dial up all the analytical skills and resources we can muster. The Marketing Ops runs the Marketing Funnel, including all marketing campaigns. This person is fluent in all marketing automation technology, and can tell you to the third decimal point how many people clicked and opened last Tuesday's email blast, how long they read it, and how many of them clicked on the product and bought it. The Marketing Ops tool kit is gigantic and growing and includes Customer Relationship Management (CRM) and marketing automation tools (Marketo, HubSpot and Salesforce).

6. Customer Support (EMT, physician/nurse)

Once you land a customer, you need to retain them and encourage them to buy more, buy more often and refer friends and family. You are intimately involved in things like customer satisfaction and immediately fixing glitches, bugs and epic failures without complaint. Your capacity for compassion and your ability to listen patiently and respond positively is paramount. This marketing role will require your highest level of interpersonal skills and emotional intelligence.

The Recycler (Turbo)

You are now in the recycling business. Once you have mastered all six marketing roles and identified, attracted and secured customers profitably, you can apply/deploy that market intelligence back into the marketing cycle, the same way an automobile engine turbocharges its performance by injecting the exaust back into the engine mechanism.

Is this the right market for you?

Is it profitable?

Are you enjoying yourself?

What are your prospects telling you?

What are the excuses/objections to buying? Is there a pattern?

Did your customers pay the price for the product that you guessed/estimated? Do they feel they are getting a fair value?

Did they use the product in the way you intended or are they using it for different purposes?

What kind of product improvements are they suggesting?

Do customers have to create any "work arounds" or patches just to get the product to work?

Are there any patterns to the customer complaints?

Are they telling others about the product? Are they willing to give you a testimonial? If not, why not?

The Technology Tailwind

Personalization is a chance to differentiate at a human scale, to use behavior as the most important clue about what people want and more important, what they need.
- Seth Godin

Today's iPhone computing power would have cost you $1 billion in 1970, according to tech entrepreneur Tom Siebel.

As a consumer, you might have a reason to be upset at the amount of your monthly phone bill. But as a business owner and entrepreneur you should be infinitely grateful.

The computing and communication tools that used to be prohibitively expensive and used only by government (Dept. of Defense, NASA) and large public corporations (GE, Exxon, P&G) are now in the palm of your hand.

The technology that won the cold war and took us to the moon is now at your disposal. Cell phone technology came from satellite technology developed by the military. The Internet was originally designed to quickly move redundant packets of information around the globe instantly after a nuclear attack.

Gordon Moore at Intel famously created Moore's Law, which asserts that semiconductor chip capacity doubles every 18 months. That means the chips are getting smaller (miniaturization) and the work cycles are even faster. These circuits create amazing amounts of heat as they work, so engineers are also designing more advanced "heat sinks" to keep chips (and devices) cool.

As these expensive corporate technologies are perfected and distributed among billions of consumers, the cost of development and distribution plummets.

Savvy developers create time-saving apps atop open source code, spreading one invention across multiple industries. As a small business, you can get lost in frenzy, but you can also benefit from these trends when you understand how to deploy the cheap tools intelligently.

A

Audience

There's an invisible thread between actor and audience, and when it's there it's stunning. There is nothing to match it.
    - Maggie Smith

As a marketer, you are like that actor on the stage. You must know your lines perfectly, and project them to the back row of the upper balcony.

The word audience derives from the same root word as "audio" and can be thought of as "the act or state of hearing, action or condition of listening"

Defining the audience is the first step in identifying your market.

I approach this as a writer, thinking about someone actually picking up my book. Who are they? What do they look like? Why do they care? How can my words make life better for them?

I visualize the individual most likely to benefit and then I expand that thinking into a group description.

When you think about Audience, it helps you define your market, approach your market and support it.

Also, don't forget your audience of Influencers. They are not your direct customers, but individuals who recommend your product, review it, or talk about it in a blog or at a barbecue.

Audience Takeaway

B

Brand

Your brand is what other people say about you when you're not in the room.
- Jeff Bezos

Ranchers used to brand their cattle permanently on the hide with a small symbol to let other ranchers know whom the cattle belonged to. The brand also allowed the shipper and the beef processor to quickly identify a cow moving to market.

Think of any consumer category (breakfast cereal, cars, shoes, fast food). There are many brands, yet one or two brands come to mind first. The same goes for B2B ("Business to Business") marketing, where brands like Microsoft (software), Accenture (professional services) dominate the landscape. Some brands like Microsoft and Delta airlines are major brands in consumer and business markets.

Your name is your personal brand. Said another way: **You, Inc**.

Your brand was formed in elementary school, and built along the way in your career. What do you people say about you? What qualities are most associated with your name?

Is the company you own (or the company you hope to start) a brand, or a "household name" yet?

Our President (whose last name is a brand), once said, "If your business is not a brand, it is a commodity." When you are a commodity (orange juice) and not a brand (Tropicana), you don't stand out on the shelf, your profit margins are lower and competitors will eat you alive.

Brand Takeaway

C
Content

Content marketing is like a first date. If you only talk about yourself, there won't be a second date.
  - David Beebe, former head of content, Marriott

It's not about you. It never was and it never will be.

Craig Davis, the former Chief Creative Officer at J. Walter Thompson, has said, "We need to stop interrupting what people are interested in and be what people are interested in."

Content should be designed around your audience, which includes your customer, your prospective customer and any Word-of-Mouth influencers who are there to help you for free.

Original content is one of the few ways to stand out in a noisy and crowded marketplace. The GEICO gecko and Flo from Progressive are examples of creative content, content that entertains and plants a seed. It's not very useful content, until you need auto insurance.

An informative blog post, a web page or a You Tube video are examples of useful content, which establish your authority in any subject area: wedding planning, catering, DJ'ing, or dance recital videos.

Never be content with your content. The moment you post or publish it, it grows stale.

A savvy marketer knows how to create content cheaply and repurpose it endlessly, on web pages, on social media and on coffee mugs and the front of goofy t-shirts.

Content Takeaway

D
Digital

End users shape the market, not technologies. Marketers need to keep up with technological developments, but more importantly, the way people respond to them. Matt Haig

In 1983, I wrote freelance feature articles on a Smith Corona electric typewriter. I used the card catalog in a library for research. "Cut and Paste" meant scissors and glue. I mailed the document to my editor and we set up our meetings using landline telephone calls.

Digital changes all that. Digital technology (personal computer, Internet, smart phone) transforms marketing as a business discipline. You can catch up quickly on your marketing competency.

Your smartphone is a supercomputer. There are thousands of digital tools available at very low cost, from social media platforms like Facebook and LinkedIn, to online research using Google and Survey Monkey, to email and marketing automation software like Constant Contact and MailChimp.

Digital is cheaper and faster. You can reach prospects at any hour of the day or any location on the planet, with all kinds of content: videos, ecommerce stores, eBooks, emails and web landing pages.

Some customers like the impersonal digital options of a call-in menu ("press 1 for the pharmacy"), a self-serve portal or a chat app. Some customers hate it and want "a real person."

The Digital Downside is when your approach (sales and service) or your content becomes impersonal or not "real." You should have a sense of when to be digital and when to be "old school": print ads, personal selling, direct mail brochures and billboards.

Sometimes it's best to just pick up the phone and call someone, or meet in person to create a meaningful conversation.

Digital Takeaway

E
Engagement

People don't want to be sold. What people want is news and information about the things they care about.
   -Larry Weber

Think about a manual shift car. You can't go anywhere until the clutch engages, and then the gears work. Your marketing is stuck in Neutral until you learn engagement.

The word "engagement" derives from "pledge" and "bind together." When you're engaged, you're not dating anymore. It's another level of commitment, with rules and expectations and payoffs. Engagement implies eventual marriage.

In marketing, you want your "suspect" customer to becoming a prospect, and then a paying, profitable customer, and then a repeat customer and word-of-mouth influencer.

Here's an engaging email you can send to me: "How to make tons of money in your 60's," "Eight Ways to be Happy as an Empty Nester" or "How to Lose Weight in December." An engaging email means people read the whole thing, and get to your Call to Action. Engaging content means we stick around to learn as much as we can. If you want people to travel to Ireland, you'd talk about flights, hotels, food, weather, pricing, and testimonials. An endless buffet of content.

Events are a terrific way to create engagement. Think of the local boat show, usually held in January and not July! Boat shows bring people together around a product and a lifestyle.

Products should be as engaging as marketing content. Design features that create trial, first-time and expert users.

Engagement Takeaway

F
Funnel

It's much easier to double your business by doubling your conversion rate than by doubling your traffic.
   - Jeff Eisenberg

The classic marketing model is known as the Funnel, known for it's "V" shape, wide at the top and narrow at the bottom. Moving a business lead through the funnel is known as "conversion." Start with a lead and turn that lead into a customer. The amount of time that takes is called the "sales cycle." For a hamburger, the sales cycle can be under a minute. For a government buying a fighter jet, it can take a decade.

Phase	Category	Behavior	Stats
Awareness	Suspect	Visits Website	100
Consideration	Prospect	Ask Questions	20
Conversion	Customer	Credit Card	5

Apply content to the Funnel precisely. For example, don't ask a Prospect (Consideration phase) for a credit card (it's too early) or refer them to your website (it's too late).

Plastic surgery is elective surgery. Most potential patients opt out after the consult in the surgeon's office, talking to the surgeon, considering elective (an expensive) medical procedure that will change their life. Plastic surgeons have billboards all over town, but they have even more content for the middle of the Funnel, because the middle is where they lose people.

Once leads become customers, don't forget how they can help you in the future. In a turbocharged engine, the exhaust is recycled into the engine to boost performance. In a turbocharged Funnel, repeat customers provide testimonials and referrals that can be pumped back into the conversion cycle.

Funnel Takeway

G
Google (and Facebook)

Google only loves you when everyone else loves you first.
–Wendy Piersall

Google and Facebook have formed what has been termed a "duopoly," a monopoly with two heavyweights instead of one. They represent 75% of all digital ad revenue and 100% of all the digital ad revenue growth.

As a marketer you should familiarize yourself with Google Search Basics, including Search Engine Optimization (SEO) a free way to get your content ranked higher. Your goal should be to show up in the top three listings for your category in your local city, or at least on page one. Anything lower than page one is a cemetery. Pay Per Click (PPC) is a Google advertising product designed to put your links next to the top search rankings. Another Google subsidiary is You Tube.

Google helps unknown companies become known, and helps customers find you when they are looking for specific knowledge, products or services. Sites like Angie's List are search aggregators for certain categories like landscaping.

Facebook is a global (and local) advertising powerhouse: 2 Billion users. Facebook works in China Grove, but not in China, where it has been declared illegal by the government.

Business marketing starts with personal marketing. Use your personal Facebook page to drive interest in your Facebook business page. You can also create individual pages for events and products. Facebook also offers a paid alternative, where you pay them to "boost" your posts.

Google (and Facebook) Takeaway

H
Hyperlocal

You won't reach as much audience, but it's the right audience - Anon.

The Mass Market is over. Cable television destroyed network television. Netflix and You Tube are destroying cable. Amazon destroyed Barnes & Noble. MP3s destroyed the music business. The fragmentation of Big #1 rolls on.

So, what's left? Millions of small opportunities, according to Chris Anderson, former Editor in Chief of *WIRED*. In "The Long Tail," Anderson suggests our culture and economy is shifting away from a focus on a relatively small number of "hits" (mainstream products and markets) at the head of the demand curve and toward a huge number of niches in the tail.

Take, ice cream, for example. If you want to dominate the number one flavor of ice cream (vanilla), good luck to you. If you're willing to own Kahlua Chocolate Crunch in York Beach Maine, you stand a good chance of dominating your category.

So, let's switch over to what this means locally. In Old School "local" marketing, you might target a particular city or several zip codes. Nowadays, you're better off targeting individual neighborhoods, or even specific blocks within a neighborhood. Think about your neighborhood. Are there not unique differences from block to block?

Taken to the extreme, hyperlocal is known as "1:1 marketing," marketing targeted at the individual level. In advertising technology, an individual smartphone can be analyzed by a remote "ad server," a rapid auction is held among advertisers and a custom ad served up, all in in 200 milliseconds. Things have become that sophisticated.

Hyperlocal Takeaway

I
Insight

A stumble may prevent a fall.
— Thomas Fuller

In the old days, the village Cleaver could look at a huge piece of granite, and say "hit it right there," and with one strike, the rock would split in two. That insight saved a lot of wasted effort chiseling rock. It's where we get our word "clever."

What if you could be more clever about your business? It would save time and money, and maybe save your business.

If I told you that your most valuable future customers all drive a Toyota Avalon, would that matter? Of course, it would. You might be more likely to befriend your local Toyota dealer or leave discount flyers only on the windshields of Avalon's in parking lots. I've picked Avalon for a reason. The average owner is in his/her early 60's and they are value purchasers (an Avalon is essentially the same car as a Lexus ES350).

Marketing insights are based on market Analytics. Analytics involves "the analysis of qualitative and quantitative data from your website, to drive continual improvement of your customers' online experience which translates into your desired outcomes (online and offline)."

Develop a Measurement Mentality. Measure everything and look for insights into what the numbers say. What time of day are customers visiting your website? How long do they stick around? What time of day do they make purchases? What part of the webpage holds their attention longest?

Use what you've learned, and make adjustments to reinforce what sells. It's called "agile marketing."

Insight Takeaway

J
Juice

A brand is no longer what we tell the consumer it is – it is what consumers tell each other it is.
 – Scott Cook

To have "juice" is slang for having market influence and the power to change consumer behavior. It's not the same as "buzz" which is fleeting. Juice is a form of electricity.

Just like the finest juice, your marketing should be "freshly squeezed" and not made from concentrate. Juice made from concentrate is a diluted product and tastes like the freezer it came from.

Your marketing materials should be fresh in the same way: up-to-date information and authentic. To many companies give us the blah-blah-blah about their product, ie no juice.

Look at the refrigerated juice section in the grocery store. There are at least ten juice brands and they all offer three to four options. Do you offer "pulp" and "pulp free" options? Look how juice brands tailored their product to the youth market with squeeze boxes.

POM is a classic marketing case study. After purchasing a pistachio orchard, entrepreneur Lynda Resnick discovered it also contained some pomegranate trees. She sponsored medical research on the health benefits of pomegranates. After receiving positive results, she decided to launch a pomegranate juice beverage. Designing the logo herself, Resnick had her team design an hourglass shape for the bottle. The POM company now offers a wide variety of products ranging from traditional pomegranate juice to pomegranate bars to coffee flavoring.

Juice Takeaway

K
Keyword

"In searching for myself, I have created myself."
— Ljupka Cvetanova, The New Land

Keywords are the words and phrases that Internet users type into the search box of a search engine, such as Google, to find what websites with matching content

. It's free on your end if you have these "key" phrases embedded in your content. When you define your company using key words, it helps you refine what you have to offer.

Let's say you're a Wedding DJ. Here's a potential hit list of 20 keywords:
1. Wedding DJ in [city name]
2. Wedding DJ packages
3. Affordable wedding DJ [city name]
4. Wedding DJ karaoke
5. Hire wedding DJ [city name]
6. DJ services [city name]
7. Country music wedding DJ
8. Wedding DJ playlist
9. Wedding DJs near [city name]
10. Professional wedding DJ [city name]
11. Wedding DJ Entertainment
12. Wedding Event DJ [city name]
13. Wedding DJ tips
14. Wedding DJ checklist
15. Wedding DJ questions
16. Wedding games for DJ
17. local DJs [city name]
18. Wedding Reception DJ
19. Wedding DJ quotes
20. Wedding DJ under 500

Keyword Takeaway

L
Listening

You have two ears and one mouth, and you should use them proportionally.
 - Susan Cain, Quiet: The Power of Introverts

Listening, not talking (or shouting) is at the very core of marketing. There is no marketing without listening. When you are talking, you can't possibly be listening.

When you find someone who truly listens, it's a rare thing. You notice that person and remember them.

I had dinner with a book publisher recently. I wanted to learn about how he goes about publishing new authors. He turned the tables on me and asked, "what are you writing these days?" His question blew me away; it was so unexpected. It means he's paying attention to his market.

Sometimes you have to distinguish the signal from the noise, to tune out the "squeaky wheel" and enjoy all the wheels that are running silently. Your low-margin, low-loyalty customers yell loudest and good customers stay silent.

Here's a tip: we listen with our eyes, not oour ears.

The human eye has more than 2 million parts, and more than a million nerve fibers connect the eye to the brain. Research shows 80% of our memories are determined by what we see; 80% of what we learn comes through our eyes.

Making eye contact is the best way to listen and share complex concepts. Look someone in the eye when you are making your case. If the other person holds your gaze, it means they are truly listening to you.

Listening Takeaway

M
Mobile

The majority of internet usage will be done via a mobile device. For most people, the mobile web will be their primary - if not their only - way of experiencing the internet.
- Peter Rojas, Co-founder of Engadget and Gizmodo

Mobile is a marketing game changer

If you haven't figured out how to go fully digital with your business, I would leapfrog right into understanding how mobile works. Jump in and master mobile design, content, functionality, search and advertising.

With mobile marketing design, you have to think about everything in much cleaner terms, because of the smaller screen size. Some design software claims to be "responsive," meaning it will format the same content for a webpage and a smartphone screen. This can only end badly.

Mobile content should recognize the small screen: more visual than text, more video over story and a lot fewer words.

Raj Aggarwal, CEO of Localytics, has remarked that the mobile trends are causing "websites to become more app-like with rich functionality."

Search and mobile advertising are also transformed. Google recently changed its search algorithm so that mobile-friendly sites have priority placement on search queries.

Smartphones are not only receivers, they transmit large amounts of information about individual interests, preferences and location. Marketers can be more specific with ad campaigns and offer more relevant options to consumers.

Mobile Takeaway

N
Niche

I didn't feel comfortable as an executive. I felt comfortable around artists and record producers... and then I found my niche: I find great producers, and I produce them.
- Jimmy Iovine, chairman of Interscope Geffen A&M; producer of albums by Bruce Springsteen, Tom Petty, U2 and Tupac; backer of Death Row Records, co-founder of Beats headphones with Dr. Dre (sold to Apple for $3 billion)

A niche ("nitch" or "neesh") is literally a shelf for fragile objects that makes them stand out.

A niche market is a smaller subset of a larger market. The niche defines product features aimed at satisfying specific market need, as well as uniquely addressing price, quality and demographics. ESPN established a niche market apart from network sports operations like CBS, ABC and NBC. Dippin' Dots are a niche market with the larger frozen dessert market.

When you identify your niche, you become a "big fish in a small pond." Niche companies are typically more profitable, with loyal customers and fewer competitors to bother them.

Interestingly, when you narrow your focus, you can gain more customers.

Three Niche Strategies:

- Use market research to find needs or wants that aren't being addressed or met by other brands or your competitors.
- Go 180 degrees from the market. Be a contrarian. Be a cable TV installer who sets exact appointment times vs. 4-hour windows.
- Make a narrow niche even narrower: golf lessons for children, but kids who have been cut from travelling soccer and baseball teams.

Niche Takeaway

O
Opportunity

If opportunity doesn't knock, build a door
— Milton Berle

I don't skate to where the puck is; I skate to where it's going.
— Wayne Gretsky

Thomas Edison said we often miss opportunity because it is disguised as work. This goes back to the Insight chapter, where we look at what the data is telling us. The people who made the most money out of the California Gold Rush were not the miners, but the "pick and shovel" vendors, men like Levi Strauss who sold them denim trousers by the trainload.

Opportunities often come disguised as customer complaints. This goes back to listening and probably how "Big and Tall" stores got started: "Why don't you have anything in my size?"

Have you set up listening posts and feedback loops in your business? What do your employees tell you about your customers? What is the business is telling you? For example, Optometrists know that if a first-time patient isn't in the dispensary within 45 minutes, that patient spends less money on eyewear for each minute delayed in the exam room.

Another skill is sizing and qualifying the opportunity. When should you make a big, bold move and when should you make a minor adjustment? A decision to increase revenue, could also reduce profit and leads to a strain on your existing resources. You might stay open an extra hour in the evening to sell more product, but you end up losing money because you have to pay more overtime and your employees burn out.

Author Seth Godin has a concept called "The Strategic Quit." A Strategic Quit is when you decide to stop pursuing an opportunity and throwing good money after bad.

Opportunity Takeaway

P
Pricing

Pricing is actually pretty simple. Customers will not pay a penny more than the true value of the product.
- Ron Johnson

Why does an automobile cost anywhere between $13,000 (Nissan Versa Note) and $4.8 million (CCXR Trevita) for essentially the same thing? Why do blueberries usually cost $3.99? Why do we pay $15 for a pasta dish at a restaurant for $1 worth of flour, water, and butter? The answer to all three questions will help you understand pricing.

What is the right price for my product?

The price or "going rate" is the amount the market will pay for whatever allows you to keep your doors open. It involves a lot of testing, a lot of trial and error.

When is offering a "freemium" a good idea?

Giving away free samples is fine, if you have a way to pay for the product ahead of time, and believe reasonably that people will pay for the product later, when they understand it.

Should I offer discounts?

Discounts and incentives can help when creating urgency, to encourage purchase or timely payment of an invoice.

Here's a tip on pricing services for consultants: cut the hours required but never cut your price (hourly rate). Your hourly rate should be *twice* what you made as an employee. If you made $38 an hour ($80k annually), you should charge $76 an hour to make it worth your while to be in business. If clients try to get you to reduce your rate, stick to your guns.

Pricing Takeaway

Q
Question

"ABC, Always be Closing"
-*Glengarry Glen Ross*

The market moves, all the time, even while you sleep. It moves even faster when you are successful; you become distracted by having real customers, paying customers and you lose your hunter instincts. You become complacent when there's enough money in the bank.

Marketers question their market assumptions daily. They question the market research. Is the research timely? Is the research valid? Can I rely on what it's telling me? Can I hire staff, sign leases and buy working materials based on it?

Ask questions of your prospects and then listen. Why are you buying this product? Would you buy my product in the future, and if so, how much would you pay for it?

Ask the same questions of your influencer network. Would your clients buy my product in the future, and if so, how much do you think they would pay for it?

Question your customers and then listen. If you are happy, will you buying again in the future? How often? Would you be willing to provide a testimonial for the product? If you're not willing, why not?

Question your competitors. If you can't do that directly, call up as a potential customer. Question your suppliers, who might also be supplying your competitors. How much longer will you be in this market? What's interesting these days?

If you're not constantly asking questions, you are not really marketing; plain and simple. Always be questioning.

Questions to Ask

R
Research

Research is what I'm doing when I don't know what I'm doing.
-Wernher von Braun

Not all research is the same. **Primary Market Research** means you are looking at the market in real-time. Primary Research can be time-consuming, messy to compile and give you false and misleading signals. People may outright lie to you or be too polite to answer the question fully. You may not have a large enough sample to make it meaningful.

Secondary Market Research is trailing data, and may be months or years old. What it lacks in timeliness, it supports with larger market samples, proven methods and predictability. Secondary market research from multiple, established sources is available through libraries for free, because the library is using taxpayer money to subscribe on behalf of individuals.

Online Research has the benefit of immediacy and trendiness, with the downside of trendiness and missing the mark widely. Some competitors may not be out in the open for strategic reasons, and this could cause you to underestimate their presence and power.

Another form of Research is known as **A/B Testing**: Which do you prefer, Product A or Product B? Which Email subject line would you open, A or B?

Online Surveys have become more popular and less expensive, including Survey Monkey and SurveyGizmo. My non-profit client recently used a primary data sampling of 236 teenagers in San Francisco to pursue $13 million in municipal grants. We cited the compelling data in all our proposals.

Research Notes

S
Storytelling

Everyone tells a story about themselves inside their own head. That story makes you what you are. We build ourselves out of that story.
- Patrick Rothfuss

We remember Fairy Tales, parables and funny anecdotes for decades but often struggle with memorizing facts and concepts, or recalling the name of someone we met five minutes ago at a party.

Storytelling is part of our deep human software. There are billions of brain cells dedicated to it, probably developed when we formed hunter-gatherer cultures in order to survive hundreds of millions of years ago. Oral traditions kept many religions alive for centuries until they could be written down.

There is a traditional story arc we know: boy meets girl, boy loses girl, boy gets girl back. There is the Cinderella Story and *Toy Story*. There are many storytelling templates. Think about advertising stories: cars make you happy, drugs make you healthy and lite beer makes you popular with your friends.

The design studio IDEO (Apple's design firm) is now offering a course called Storytelling for Influence, recognizing the power of stories. Big companies like GE, Nissan and Microsoft are hiring journalists and editors and building internal newsrooms. Why would they do something like that?

Marketers understand the critical need to collect, refine and tell their stories, over and over and over again.

A happy customer is a story. A customer testimonial is a story. Getting a loan from a family member (or from the bank) is a story. What is your story? Are you telling it?

My Story

T
Targets

This is what I call a target-rich environment.
- Maverick, *Top Gun* (1986)

Drug Discovery companies like to say they take "multiple shots on goal." This is a hockey/soccer sports analogy that acknowledges you are going to miss a shot most times, but you give yourself the opportunity for that one lucky shot to find the goal. This means you create and offer multiple products or you go after a broader market, with many targets in it.

Target Marketing means breaking a market into segments and then concentrating marketing efforts a few key segments consisting of customers whose needs and desires most closely match your products or services. You can have more than one target, and each should receive their own customized set of messages.

Speaking of targets, what can small companies learn from a discount retailer like **Target**? They have clean, bright stores in convenient locations and a cute bullseye dog mascot in their ads. The company started out as Goodfellow Dry Goods in June 1902. The first Target discount store opened in 1962. They are the second largest retailer next to Target. They now offer groceries and broke up with Amazon to form Target.com

Retargeting, also known as remarketing, is a form of online advertising that can help you keep your brand in front of bounced traffic after they leave your website. For most websites, only 2% of web traffic converts on the first visit. Retargeting is a tool designed to help companies reach the 98% of users who don't convert right away. Retargeting uses cookie technology to follow your prospects. Some might call this "stalking" and it's a negative for your brand.

Target Takeaway

U
User Generated Content(UGC)

The next wave of the Web is going to be user-generated content.
- John Doerr, Kleiner Perkins Caufield & Byers

UGC is simple and it's free. Don't overlook its value.

UGC is just one example of the "democratization" of content production. Traditionally, "gatekeepers" like newspaper editors, publishers and news shows approved all content and information before it was aired or published.

Now technology cuts out the gatekeepers, as billions of individuals worldwide are able to post text, digital photos and digital videos online.

Brands are increasingly becoming more focused on incorporating UGC into their promotions. When brands showcase their customers' fan art and testimonials, it builds a positive relationship and shows users that companies care. Or at least they're making the effort to pretend to care.

REI Co-op ran a terrific UGC campaign several years ago on social media. They asked customers to post pictures of places in nature where they were using REI products such as hiking boots, backpacks and kayaks. REI also placed a premium on spotlighting photographs that had very high production quality, so the campaign attracted outdoor enthusiasts and professional photographers who wanted exposure on REI's site.

REI has 1.8 million followers on its Facebook page. Another marketing strategy is for a small business to post content on a large company page, in what is called the "halo effect."

How I will Use UGC

V
Viral

The first lesson in constructing viral content is having the strength, courage, and self-confidence to get in touch with your own feelings, thinking about what profoundly affects you.
- Ken Poirot

Marketers dream of having their video going viral or their infographic going viral They dream of the day something inconsequential thye post becomes the lead item on *Reddit or Buzzfeed*, or the evening news.

There's no formula at all for what makes something viral. The Internet is unpredictable, by design. You can't "game" it and you can't game Google. If anyone promises you they can make something go viral, they are lying to you.

There's also an operational side of viral. If you are lucky enough to have something about your product or company go viral (in a good way), are you prepared for the attention.

Can your web server handle the increased traffic? Can you fulfill the orders and deal with all the customer service issues?

And if something negative gets out there in a big way, are you ready for that? Do you have a "damage control" plan in place?

Once something is on the Internet, it is everywhere and it is there forever. You'll never be able to scrub it clean across the board.

Luckily, consumers have a short attention span and you will be forgotten in the next news cycle.

Viral Takeaway

W

Wants v. Needs

One can never have enough socks.
-Dumbledore, Harry Potter & the Sorcerer's Stone

Marketers traditionally appeal to Wants (optional) versus Needs (required) like food, clothing, shelter and health. It could also be said there are items in the Needs category that are merely Wants: ice cream, flip-flops, vacation houses and elective surgery.

Relying on distraction, marketers appeal to short-term pleasure (brain chemical - dopamine) versus long-term happiness (brain chemical serotonin).

Grocery and retail stores are designed for pleasure. Many of them resemble theme parks (IKEA especially). Online shopping is almost purely about short-term pleasure and immediate gratification. Google Search rewards commercial sites with fast page loads.

Advertisers can use crowbars and levers to get consumers "off the dime" with phenomenon like "Keeping Up with the Joneses" and FOMO (Fear of Missing Out." Advertiser catch phrases include "Act Now!", "while supplies last," and only three tickets left" on web travel sites.

So, how many pair of socks (or shoes) do you really need? Five? Seven? Fourteen?

Where does your product or service fit into the Wants v. Needs continuum?

Are you selling ice to Eskimos or books to college professors? Are you "pushing a piece of string?" Or, are you selling something essential and "mission critical"?

It helps to know the difference.

Wants v. Needs

X
Xerox

Gutenberg made everybody a reader. Xerox made everyone a publisher.
- Marshall McLuhan

Xerox changed how we do business. Formerly you put carbon paper between sheets of paper in a typewriter, or you used a mimeograph machine. The copier machine was so revolutionary that the company name became a verb with common usage. To "Xerox something" meant you were going to copy it. The same phenomenon has happened to Google and Uber. Will your brand have this kind of impact?

Xerox PARC was a research and development facility responsible for the development of laser printing, the modern personal computer and the graphical user interface. It's the place where Steve Jobs got the idea for the computer mouse. Unfortunately, Xerox's industrial "business to business" B2B magic has not translated into a consumer brand.

In marketing, it's advantageous to be a constant copier. Copy other businesses' best practices including marketing. Take advantage of the "halo effect" of borrowing from other peoples' content. It's not stealing as long as you ask for permission and give proper attribution when you do it. It's not only flattering, it extends the brand of the individual or the company when you list it on your website or link to it.

. It's also advantageous to copy or repurpose your marketing content across blogs, website pages and social media posts. It reduces the cost of developing content and reinforces a consistent message. People are way too busy these days. They won't remember reading the same words in several places.

Xerox Takeaway

Y

YouTube

I go on YouTube when somebody says to look something up.
- George Clooney

YouTube is another example of technology "consumerization."

Suddenly everyone can be a movie producer or own the equivalent of a television station or a cable channel with very little cost.

YouTube is owned by Google, so it runs on a search engine. YouTube became so popular that Facebook wanted in on the game with Facebook Live.

Google claims that more than one-third of all Internet users watch YouTube and more than half of those views now come from mobile devices. Pay attention. This is your audience.

The Internet is a perfect platform for sharing basic information, and by extension, it's becoming ideal for posting training videos.

It's no surprise that the Web is awash in training and coaching videos, from cooking to exercise, academic lectures to playing a musical instrument. There is probably a video tutorial out there for anything you care to learn.

If you are an expert at doing something or possess a special set of skills, and are willing to help other people try their hand at that particular thing or improve their skill, there is no better way to do it than to make your own video tutorial and share it on the Internet.

Not all tutorials are created equal. Make sure your video is informative, professional and thorough. The production quality of the video will reflect the quality of your product or service.

My YouTube Channel

Z

Zero Cost Marketing

Capital isn't scarce; vision is
-Sam Walton

The concept of guerrilla marketing was invented by Jay Conrad Levinson in a book of the same name. Guerrilla Marketing means using an unconventional system of promotions that relies on time, energy and imagination rather than a big marketing budget.

Here are a few examples of zero-cost guerilla marketing:

If you are already paying rent on a building, do more with it. Treat it like a billboard. Give a local artist some free drawing space by letting him use his artistry on your shutters or paint a mural on the side of your Building. Create Projections onto a blank wall at night and it becomes a natural billboard and cinema screen.

Offer free exhibition space on your premises to new edgy performance artists, a performance school looking for practice space or Design students. You will be getting some amazing visual merchandising for free that may spread via word of mouth.

If you need to trial a regional market or neighborhood or need to sell on a seasonal basis, try a "pop-up" location or rent out an unused space cheaply to help someone else lower their rent.

Learn to barter products and services with other related (or un-related businesses), such as a health-food store and a fitness gym joining forces, or a gym teaming up with an auto mechanic (free two-hour gym membership while your car is worked on).

You should also know when to bootstrap and when to spend money. Sites like Fiverr mean you can spend $40 on graphic design versus thousands of dollars. Hint: your designer may be in Macedonia, not Mebane.

Zero Cost/Bootstrapping Ideas

Further Reading

Anderson, Chris, *The Long Tail*

Beckwith, Harry, *Selling the Invisible*

Berger, Jonah, *Contagious: Why Things Catch On*

Dib, Allan, *The 1-Page Marketing Plan: Get New Customers, Make More Money, And Stand out From The Crowd*

Godin, Seth, *Permission Marketing; Purple Cow; Tribes; Free Prize Inside*

Holiday, Ryan, *Growth Hacker Marketing*

Jantsch, John, *Duct Tape Marketing*

Levinson, Jay Conrad, *Guerilla Marketing; Social Media Guerilla Marketing*

Lindstrom, Martin, *Buy-ology*

Westergaard, Nick, *Get Scrappy*

Jon Obermeyer is a native of Santa Barbara, CA. He holds a degree in English from Westmont College, an MFA in Creative Writing from UNC Greensboro and the Basic Certificate in Economic Development from UNC Chapel Hill.

Jon has advised over 1,500 start-ups in his career as a banker, economic developer, and seed fund CEO. A recent resident of San Francisco, Jon co-launched an internal creative agency at Hearst Digital Media's SFGate website and co-founded a technology marketing agency producing original content for SanDisk and Samsung.

Jon was formerly Director of Marketing for Astadia, a global Cloud computing IT consulting firm that was backed by Kodiak Ventures. With Astadia Chief Technology Officer Mike Lingo, he co-authored the first business book on cloud computing *Hey! You! Get Onto My Cloud* (2010).

He has worked in executive roles at venture-backed companies, ran national initiatives for the Wake Forest University Institute of Regenerative Medicine, and formerly owned a convention services/trade show business supporting 180 events annually.

A professional writer since 2002, Jon has edited or co-authored seven business books on the topics of cloud computing, the human immune system, angel investing, customer service, project management, social media selling and artificial intelligence/machine learning.

A lifelong creative, Jon is a published poet, short story writer and essayist, with six books of creative work available on Amazon.

He lives in Durham, NC.

www.ingramcontent.com/pod-product-compliance
Lightning Source LLC
Chambersburg PA
CBHW050239230526
45470CB00005B/2019